D1085122

A partnership between American Library Association
and FINRA Investor Education Foundation

FINRA is proud to support the American Library Association

A TEEN GUIDE TO INVESTING

A TEEN GUIDE TO

Buying Mutual
FUNDS

MARYLOU
MORANO
KJELLE

Mitchell Lane
PUBLISHERS

P.O. Box 196
Hockessin, DE 19707
www.mitchelllane.com

A TEEN GUIDE TO INVESTING

Investment Options for Teens
A Teen Guide to Buying Stocks
A Dividend Stock Strategy for Teens
A Teen Guide to Buying Bonds
A Teen Guide to Buying Mutual Funds
A Teen Guide to Safe-Haven Savings

Printing 1 2 3 4 5 6 7 8 9

Library of Congress
Cataloging-in-Publication Data
Kjelle, Marylou Morano.
  A teen guide to mutual funds / by Marylou Morano Kjelle.
    pages cm.—(A teen guide to investing)
  Includes bibliographical references and index.
  Audience: Grade 7 to 8.
  ISBN 978-1-61228-427-9 (library bound)
  1. Mutual funds—Juvenile literature. 2. Investments—Juvenile literature. 3. Finance, Personal—Juvenile literature. I. Title.
  HG4530.K58 2014
  332.63'27—dc23
                                        2013012290

eBook ISBN: 9781612284897

PLB

Contents

Whether it's choosing a video game or deciding on an investment, carefully weighing all your options will help you make the right decision.

A "Mutually Agreeable" WAY TO INVEST

A new video game has just been released and you would really like to have it. There's just one problem: It costs $90 and you've saved up only $45. Your brother and sister want the game also, but they have even less money than you. Each of you is unable to purchase the video game on your own, but when you combine your savings (your brother has $30 and your sister has $15), you now have enough capital, or money, to buy the game.

When you purchase something, whether it is a video game, a bike, or a car, you are putting money into, or investing in, that object. Your capital undergoes a change from the money in your pocket to whatever it is you've purchased. In this example, your cash (and that of your brother and sister) became the video game. This object now has a specific value or worth to you because it represents the $90 it took to purchase it. Another way of looking at it would be to say that the video game has become a "container" that holds your $90.

One way to get more money to invest is to pool your money with others. This is how mutual funds work. When many people combine their money, each investor owns a small share of a large investment.

Investing in mutual funds is a little like combining your money with that of your siblings and purchasing a video game. Like the video game, a mutual fund is also a container that holds investments that are shared by many people. When you, your brother, and your sister combined your money, you had more to spend and therefore you were able to purchase the video game. Pooling your money in this way increased your purchasing power. Each contributor, in the end, was able to buy a part of something that he or she would not have been able to afford alone.

When people purchase mutual funds they also pool their money, only now their combined capital is used to purchase other investments like stocks, bonds, and real estate. These financial assets are also called securities. A single mutual fund might be shared by thousands of investors and be worth billions of dollars in assets.

The video game you and your siblings purchased belongs to all three of you. Each investor owns a piece of the game. In a similar way, a person who invests in a mutual fund owns a piece of the fund. In the investment world, a piece of an investment is called a share, and the person who owns the share is called a shareholder. The price of a share varies from mutual fund to mutual fund, and can range from a few dollars to several hundred. The price of one mutual fund share is called the fund's net asset value (NAV). NAV is calculated each day at the end of the business day, using a formula. The total value of the fund's investments, minus its expenses, is divided by the total number of shares owned by the investors. The result, in dollars, is what it would cost to buy one share of the mutual fund. This is also the dollar amount you would receive if you sold one share of the fund. The total value of a person's mutual fund investment is calculated by multiplying the NAV by the number of shares the person owns. A fund's NAV changes regularly because the value of the securities within the fund changes every day.

Some mutual funds, called closed-end mutual funds, limit the number of shares they will issue to investors. If you want to purchase shares in this type of mutual fund, you will need to wait until an existing shareholder is ready to redeem, or sell, their shares. Closed-end mutual funds are only sold through a broker. In contrast, open-end mutual funds do not limit the number of shares that can be bought and sold, and the shares can be bought directly from a mutual fund company, like the Vanguard Group. Most mutual funds are open-end funds.

People invest money for many reasons, but most would agree that the main purpose of investing is to make more money, either for now or the future. The profits earned by a mutual fund are shared with all the investors of the fund. Mutual funds earn money in two ways: when dividends are earned, and when the NAV increases.

Like a tender young plant, carefully nurtured investments will thrive and grow. One way to make money grow quicker is to reinvest any profits earned by the investment back into the mutual fund.

Dividends are regular income payments that come from the profits of the companies that the mutual fund has invested in. Payment of dividends varies, according to the mutual fund. Dividends can be paid monthly, quarterly, semi-annually, or annually. Many investors reinvest, or put their dividends back into their mutual fund, by buying more shares. Reinvesting makes their money grow even faster.

An investor also makes money when the NAV price increases. This occurs when the value of the security has increased, but the fund manager, the person who oversees the fund, has not sold the security. The investor's profit is called an unrealized gain until their shares are actually sold. If the NAV drops, there can also be an unrealized loss. These gains or losses become actual, or realized, gains or losses when the investor sells his or her shares.

It is also important to note that when a mutual fund sells shares of a stock for a gain, that money must be distributed to its shareholders. This doesn't mean the shareholders actually made money, however, because when this happens, the NAV drops by the same amount.

For example, let's say you currently have 100 shares with a NAV of $10—your investment is worth $1,000. Your mutual fund sells shares of stock and distributes $1 in capital gains per share, or $100. A capital gain is the increase in value, or profit, realized when an asset is sold. The NAV is now lower—$9 per share, to be exact. Your 100 shares are now worth $900 and you have $100 in cash. Most investors choose to reinvest their capital gains distributions back into the fund. With your $100 distribution, you can now buy 11.11 more shares of the mutual fund, giving you a total of 111.11 shares at $9 each—worth $1,000. While this might not seem like a big deal, you will be responsible for capital gains taxes on the distribution you received. You will eventually owe less taxes when you sell your mutual fund shares, but this could be a long time from now if you are investing for the long term.

Capital gains, and their unexpected taxes, can cut into the profits made by mutual funds.

COMPANY GROWTH

You can see how well a mutual fund has performed in the past by reading the company's prospectus. Once you have purchased your own shares, it is wise to continue to monitor the fund's growth. Many economic factors affect performance, and how a fund has performed in the past does not guarantee how it will perform in the future.

The type of mutual fund a person invests in depends on their goals. Growth funds seek out and invest in rapidly growing companies. These companies are often new, so growth funds are considered somewhat risky. Over the short term, these funds can fluctuate in price quite a bit, but the possible long-term gains are what investors are hoping for. These funds are best suited for people who can afford to wait for their money to grow.

The managers of value funds look for companies that they believe are undervalued and invest in them. When a stable company encounters a temporary or minor problem, its share price will often drop. Mutual funds that invest in such companies are called value funds. The managers of value funds look for companies that they believe are undervalued and invest in them. If a value fund manager feels that a

A "Mutually Agreeable" Way to Invest

INVESTOR TRIVIA

Do the Math: Based on average returns, if you invest $2,000 into a mutual fund when you are eighteen years old, and add another $2,000 again each year when you are nineteen, twenty, and twenty-one, you will have over $1 million by the time you are ready to retire at age sixty-five, even if you never add another penny of your own money.

stock is selling for less than what it should, he or she will buy it, hoping that it will eventually rise to its fair value. This type of mutual fund is usually less volatile than a growth fund, so investors looking for a less risky fund may prefer this type.

The financial world offers many different ways to invest money. Mutual funds are just one way. Is a mutual fund a "mutually agreeable" investment option for you? Let's take a closer look and find out.

Are you ready to jump into the world of mutual fund investments?

A financial plan is one of the most important plans you can make. Planning alone, however, is not enough. You've got to put your plan into action.

CHAPTER 2

What's Your (FINANCIAL) PLAN?

You make plans with friends for the weekend. You help your family plan a vacation. You are probably, right now, planning the steps needed to continue your education after high school. There are no two ways about it. Life requires a lot of planning, and one of the most important plans anyone can make is a financial plan. Like the itinerary of a vacation, a financial plan gets you thinking about how you have managed your finances in the past, (where have you been?), and what your financial situation is at the present time (where are you now?). Most importantly, a financial plan helps guide your financial future by helping you set goals to achieve within a certain time frame (where would you like to go?). You should have a financial plan in place before you invest in a mutual fund, or any other financial investment.

It's not difficult to create a financial plan. You can do it with paper and pencil, or you can use a computer. What you'll need most is time—time to think about how you have handled your finances in the past and what financial goals you would like to accomplish in the future. You'll also need time to read and learn about different investment tactics, and time to consider which investment strategy is the best for you. Information about investing is available from investment companies on their websites. Your public library also has books about personal finance and money management. Most expenses come due, or have to be paid, at least once every thirty days, so many people use a month as the basis for their financial plan. Taking control of your finances is fun, but it is serious business, too. There are several things to consider when creating a financial plan.

Many mutual fund companies have a website. You can use the Internet to learn about investments, research various mutual funds, and even make online investments.

First, you'll want to assess your income: do you have an income, or money that comes to you on a regular basis? Many young people have a small, but consistent flow of money from an allowance or odd jobs, like yard work or babysitting. Other teens have more substantial income from part-time work in a store or fast-food restaurant. It is important to ask yourself if your income covers all your necessary expenses.

For one month, keep a careful record of your income. Make sure you include money coming from all sources, but only consider the money you can count on. For example, the part-time job at the corner convenience store where you work fifteen hours every week is dependable income. On the other hand, the $100 you receive each year in gifts for your birthday is not dependable. Since your birthday doesn't come every month, don't include this money when you are planning a budget. Money received for your birthday and other special occasions is extra money—it's great to receive, but shouldn't be counted on to pay expenses.

Expenses are the things we spend our money on. They fall into two categories, necessary and unnecessary, and they are different for each person. Young people usually live with their parents or other adults who support them, but living situations vary. In most cases, the adult provides the money for necessary expenses like food, shelter, health insurance, and other things that a teen needs. Still, a young person who is supported by an adult may be asked to contribute some money towards personal expenses, such as clothing, a cell phone bill, or gasoline, if he or she drives the family car. In other situations, caregivers may help with these expenses, but require their teen to pay for other expenses like going out with friends, cosmetics, haircuts, or movie and video game rentals.

The best way to see how you are spending money is to write down everything you purchase, no matter how small the amount. Divide your expenses into necessary and unnecessary. Expenses have a way of adding up, which is why you must account for every cent. The dollar you spend on a can of soda every day as you walk home from school may not seem like much, but it adds up to a few hundred dollars a year. Many teens don't know how or where they spend their money. They just know that they do! Listing your expenses will show you where your money goes.

Now that you know your income and your expenses, you can create a budget. A budget is a snapshot look at your finances. It will help you determine if you have enough income to cover your expenses. Is there any money left over at the end of the month? If so, you are earning more than you spend, which is a good thing. On the other hand, do you ever find yourself short on money? Do you often borrow money from a friend, sibling, or parent? If this is the case, your expenses are greater than your income. To put it another way, you spend more than you earn.

If you use every penny you earn on your expenses, or if you frequently run out of money before you pay for all your expenses, you will have to make some financial adjustments before considering investing in a mutual fund or any other investment. You can't invest money you don't have, so you will need to figure out a way to make some extra money to invest.

There are only two ways to get extra money. You can either earn more income or cut back on your expenses. Each investor must decide this for himself or herself. You may already be working the maximum amount of hours you can work and still have sufficient time for school work and the other things you do. In this case, it is nearly impossible to earn more income unless you can find a job that pays more money per hour. Likewise, you may be spending all of the money you earn on things you really need. In this case, there are no expenses that can be cut from your spending. Regardless of where the changes are made, the goal of a budget is to get your expenses to be less than, or at least equal to, your income.

Before investing in a mutual fund or another investment, you should have some money set aside for an emergency in case you lose your income, either temporarily or long term. If you became sick and couldn't

Saving money in a piggy bank or even a bank account may seem like the safest way to keep from losing your money. But mutual funds and other investments can offer a much greater opportunity for your money to grow.

work for a week, where would you get the money you need to cover your expenses? Financial experts recommend that you have three to six months' worth of expenses saved in an emergency account. Then, if something unexpected happens, you could use this emergency cushion to cover your bills. It isn't wise to invest money in a mutual fund (or any other investment) that you might need to cover your day-to-day expenses or any other needs.

After you have worked on your budget and calculated how much money to set aside in an emergency fund, you will have a good idea of how much money you have left to invest. Now it's time to consider your financial goals. Many common reasons for investing, such as

Carefully investing your money now will pay off in the future and help you save the money you need to meet your financial goals, like purchasing a car or traveling the world.

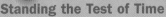

INVESTOR TRIVIA

Standing the Test of Time

Mutual funds were first used in the eighteenth-century Netherlands. The first mutual fund in the United States was called the Massachusetts Investors Trust. It was organized in Boston in 1924, and survived the stock market crash of 1929. It is still accepting investments today and is managed by a company known as MFS Investment Management.

purchasing a house or saving for retirement, may not seem very important right now because they are far in the future. As a teenager, you are at an advantage if you plan for these things now. But you can also invest to pay for college, a car, or traveling. Your financial plan should also take into consideration your larger financial picture. Do you have other investments? What are your plans for that money?

There are many variables that should be considered when creating a financial plan. Also keep in mind that a financial plan isn't fixed. It will change as your life changes. Completing your education, establishing a career, and growing older are just a few of the things that will affect and change your financial plan. The financial plan you create ten years from now will look much different from the one you create today. And the financial plan you create today will make managing your money easier in the years to come.

The economy experiences both rough seas and calm waters, but historically, mutual funds have been good investments that have stood the test of time.

CHAPTER 3

Types of
MUTUAL FUNDS

Since a mutual fund is a container that holds other investments, it is grouped by the type of security it contains. The most common mutual funds are stock, bond, and money market mutual funds, but there are other types as well, including mutual funds that hold a combination of securities and others that invest in foreign countries and their industries. The different industries that make up the parts of the economy are called sectors. Some examples of sectors are business, healthcare, and real estate. Some mutual funds invest in individual sectors, but this could be risky, since the investment relies heavily on the success or failure of one industry. The collection of investments within a mutual fund is called a portfolio.

Stock Funds

Corporations need capital to improve their products, expand work space, and hire new employees. One of the ways a company raises capital

Purchasing shares of stock in a company is like sharing a large pie with other investors. The size of your "slice" is determined by how much money you have to invest and the value of the company.

is by selling stock. A stock is a piece of a company that you can purchase. Similar to a mutual fund, each piece is called a share. Stock prices range from a few pennies to several hundred dollars a share. A company must be publicly held in order to sell its stock to the general public. Some of the largest corporations in the United States, like the healthcare giant Johnson & Johnson or the technology leader Microsoft, are publicly held corporations.

Anyone with enough money can buy stock and become a partial owner of a publicly held company. Even purchasing one share gives an investor ownership in a company. As an owner, the shareholder is entitled to a fraction, or small part, of the company's assets and earnings. The more profitable the company, the more valuable its stock is. However, the value of stocks fluctuates, which makes them a volatile investment. Therefore, investing in stocks poses some risk. For example, if a company runs into financial trouble, the price of its stock will reflect the problem and might decrease in value. And if the economy as a whole runs into trouble, the prices of most, if not all, stocks could decrease. On the other hand, if a company grows and becomes more profitable, the price of its stock will increase, and the overall investment will be worth more money. Despite their volatility, over long periods of time stocks have generally outperformed, or made more money than, other investments. Stocks are growth-oriented investments. There are no guarantees, but historical data shows that over long periods of time, the values of stocks increase on average. Stocks, as well as bonds, described below, are traded (bought and sold) on the stock market, which is also called the stock exchange.

The companies mutual funds invest in are labeled according to their size. Large-cap companies are those whose stock market values are over $10 billion. Small-cap companies are valued at less than $2 billion, and mid-cap companies fall in the middle.

Not only is Walmart a publicly traded large-cap company, it is also the largest retailer in the United States.

Bond Funds

A bond is a loan. You give a government or a company your money and they promise to pay it back. A Treasury bond is a loan made to the United States government to help pay for national expenses. A municipal bond is money loaned to a city, state, or local municipality to raise money to build roads, bridges, and other municipal structures. A corporation issues bonds to expand its business. In every case, the money is loaned for a specified period of time at a specified interest rate. The higher the interest rate, the more money you make.

Bonds are not entirely risk-free, but they are safer than stocks. There is always the chance that the government, municipality, or company will default on the loan, or not pay you back. The greater the chance of this happening, the greater the rate of interest the receiver of the loan is willing to pay you for loaning your money. For example, government bonds, like Treasury bonds, are considered very safe because they are backed by the "full faith and credit" of the United States government. There is little likelihood of the government going out of business and defaulting on its loan. This investment poses little risk; therefore, the interest rate on government bonds is lower than on other bonds, like corporate bonds. The interest rate on a bond is also dependent on the length of time you agree to loan your money. Bonds have a maturity date. This is the agreed-on date that your money will be returned to you. Although definitions vary, short-term bonds are usually bonds that mature in less than five years. Intermediate-term bonds mature in five to ten years and long-term bonds mature in ten years or longer. The longer the time period to maturity, the higher the interest rate your bond will earn.

A bond fund invests in many different bonds, and the fund manager is dedicated to researching the risks and returns of these bonds. For these reasons, a bond fund could offer better returns with less risk than putting your money into a single bond.

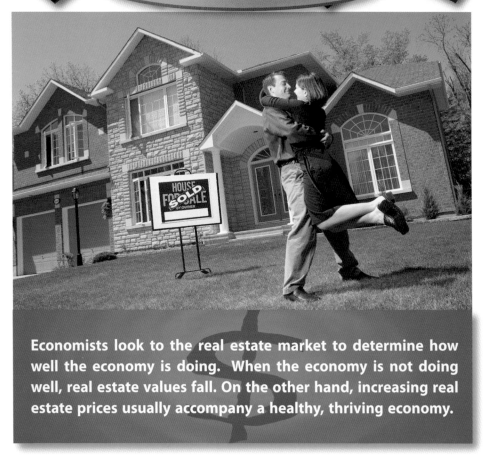

Economists look to the real estate market to determine how well the economy is doing. When the economy is not doing well, real estate values fall. On the other hand, increasing real estate prices usually accompany a healthy, thriving economy.

Real Estate

Real estate is land, the air above it, and any buildings or structures that stand on it. Residential real estate is land with homes, apartments, or other types of housing buildings standing on it, or land set aside for such buildings. Commercial real estate consists of stores, restaurants, and other businesses. Commercial real estate exists in areas that are set aside for commerce, or the buying and selling of goods.

The health of the economy is often determined by how well the real estate market is doing. Historically, real estate as an investment has produced average returns of about 8 to 10 percent a year. But in a down economy, the price of real estate usually falls. Because of their volatility, mutual funds that invest in the real estate sector should be long-term investments.

Money Market Funds

Money market funds invest in short-term, low-risk investments, like US Treasury bills, certificates of deposit (CDs) and top-rated, short-term debt issued by corporations. Money market funds are liquid investments; they can normally be cashed in at any time and still be profitable. They are also safer investments than stocks, bonds, and real estate. Because of their safety and liquidity, the yield on money market funds is not as high as some other investments. On the plus side, you don't need a lot of money to invest in them. Although minimum investment amounts vary, you can often purchase a money market fund with as little as $500.

Sometimes people use money market funds as a place to hold their money while they decide on another investment for their funds. In most cases, all you need to do to get your money out of this investment is write a check or transfer the money from your mutual fund account to your bank account. Although their names are similar, a money market fund is not the same as a money market account offered by a bank, which is a type of savings account that is usually insured by the government's Federal Deposit Insurance Corporation (FDIC).

Precious Metal Funds

Precious metal funds invest in gold and other precious metals. Investing in these commodities is risky because the price of precious metals tends to do the exact opposite of the stock market. For example, if the stock market goes up, the price of precious metals decreases. Still, having a small investment in precious metals in your portfolio is considered a good idea, as it will offset any decrease in stock prices.

Index Funds

Some mutual funds are designed to match the performance of the stock market. This is called "indexing." The portfolios of these funds, which are called index funds, are based on stock market standards. One of the most commonly tracked standards is the Standard & Poor's 500 stock market index (S&P 500). This is a list of five hundred large

Stocks . . . bonds . . . government securities . . . mutual funds. It's easy to get lost in the investment world. Learn all you can about an investment before you take the plunge and invest your money.

American companies weighted by size. Many financial analysts consider the performance of the S&P index to represent the overall health of the stock market. Like a stock fund, an index fund allows an investor to own a small piece of a lot of corporations that trade on the US stock market. And since an index fund tracks a stock market index, it does not have to be actively managed. Over long periods of time, index funds often make more money than traditional, actively managed mutual funds. One final advantage of index funds is that the costs associated with them are lower than with other mutual funds. Typically, the expenses of an index fund are about 0.2 percent of the fund's assets.

Exchange-Traded Funds (ETFs)

Another investment that tracks indexes is the exchange-traded fund (ETF). An ETF is similar to an index fund, but it trades like a stock on the stock market. ETFs can be bought at any time during the day when the stock market is open. This means that an investor can purchase an ETF at a decreased price when the market is at the day's low point. This is not true with an index fund. No matter when you purchase or sell an index fund, the cost (and profit) is determined by the fund price listed at the end of the business day.

One disadvantage of ETFs is cost. Management costs are typically higher than index funds. Because ETFs are bought and sold on the stock exchange, they can't always be purchased directly. If you use a broker to purchase an ETF, you will pay a broker's commission every time you buy or sell shares. The price of ETFs also varies. When they are in demand, their price rises and when there is excess, their price drops. Some ETFs track individual sectors instead of tracking a broader index

Financial advisors are specially trained to help you find an investment that is right for you. They can be very helpful, but be sure you know how they will be paid. Some will charge a flat or hourly fee, while others only make money (or a commission) when they sell various investments. While it may seem more expensive to pay a flat fee, some experts warn against using commission-based advisors, because they could sell products that make them more money instead of the investments that are best for their clients.

like the S&P 500 or the Dow Jones Industrial Average (DJIA), making them riskier investments.

One of the ways mutual funds grow and increase in value is through reinvestment, or putting earned money back into the fund. This means keeping whatever income is earned by the mutual fund in the mutual fund. Reinvestment allows your mutual fund to increase in value and grow larger with time.

There are several companies that rate mutual funds and report on how well they are performing (earning money). Morningstar is one of the most commonly used. This company rates mutual funds based on stars, with five stars being the highest. Morningstar looks at a mutual fund's performance after taking into consideration risk and the overall health of the investment. Morningstar does not recommend the purchase of a mutual fund based on its rating alone. It offers information that helps an investor decide if a particular mutual fund should be further researched. Other companies like Lipper and Zacks offer mutual fund ratings as well.

Mutual fund investments range from very safe (for example, money market funds) to very risky (for example, stock funds). It is important to remember that just because an investment did well in the past, there is no guarantee that it will do well in the future.

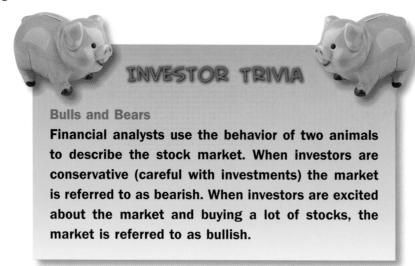

INVESTOR TRIVIA

Bulls and Bears
Financial analysts use the behavior of two animals to describe the stock market. When investors are conservative (careful with investments) the market is referred to as bearish. When investors are excited about the market and buying a lot of stocks, the market is referred to as bullish.

Many investments, including mutual funds, have the potential to lose money. If you don't like the idea of risking your money, a safer investment, like an FDIC-insured savings account, may be for you.

CHAPTER 4

The Pros and Cons of
MUTUAL FUNDS

The best way to determine if investing in mutual funds is right for you is to look at the pros and cons of the investment. We'll consider the advantages first, then look at the negative aspects of mutual funds.

In Chapter Three, we saw that mutual funds differ in the type of securities they represent. One mutual fund may invest in only one type of security, like stocks or bonds, while another may invest in a combination of securities. Since a mutual fund typically invests in twenty-five to one hundred or more securities, owning a mutual fund is like owning a tiny piece of a lot of different investments. Many people are attracted to this diversification because it balances their risk. If one security within a mutual fund decreases in value and loses money, the loss could be evened out by another security's increase in value.

Managing investments takes time, but you don't have to spend a lot of time monitoring mutual funds because the funds hire people to do the managing for you. These managers and the researchers who help them work full time analyzing securities before they decide what to purchase, sell, or hold for a mutual fund's portfolio. They look at a security's profits, losses, assets, and liabilities. They study the company's products and its competition. They read reports and other literature about the company and its industry. They use their judgment to buy and sell the securities that meet the needs of their investors. This oversight is an important reason people invest in mutual funds.

A fund manager must be qualified to oversee a mutual fund. Usually this person has gone to business school and may have further business and financial qualifications. A fund manager also has many years' experience working with investments. Since investment decisions are up to the fund manager and his or her team, you will want to research the experience and past performance of the people in charge of any fund you're considering investing in.

Money invested in mutual funds typically produces a better rate of return when kept long term than money placed in a bank account. The interest on money kept in a bank account is largely controlled by the Federal Reserve System, which is the main banking system of the United States. The money earned (or lost) by a mutual fund is determined by the securities themselves and how well they perform in the economy.

Many mutual funds are no-load, or commission-free investments. This means the fund doesn't charge an investor to purchase or redeem shares. Some funds, however, charge a front-end load, which is a commission paid at the time the mutual fund is purchased, or a back-end load, which is a commission paid when the mutual fund is sold.

Mutual funds are regulated by a government agency called the Securities and Exchange Commission (SEC). The SEC requires a mutual fund to release certain information to its investors. This report, called a prospectus, includes information about a fund's securities, including how well the fund has performed over its history, how much it costs to

The Securities and Exchange Commission is a government agency that protects investors by enforcing laws that regulate investments.

run the fund, and how quickly securities are turned over (bought and sold).

You don't need a lot of money to invest in mutual funds. Most mutual funds have an investment minimum of between $500 and $1000. Some require even less than this.

A mutual fund meets many different types of investment needs. Whether an investor wants a short-term or long-term investment, a steady stream of income to use now, or a way to accumulate money for the future, there is a mutual fund to meet this need.

Investing in mutual funds is relatively easy. Depending on the type of mutual fund you invest in, you can open up a fund account either by mail or online at the mutual fund company's website. You can increase your investment by mailing additional checks or transferring money from an existing account. Most mutual fund companies have a toll-free telephone number and a website, so it's easy to contact them. Some have local branch offices that you can visit. You can usually sign up for online account access to track the progress of your investments.

Redeeming your shares is easy also. You may be able to do this through your online account; if not, all you need to do is to contact the mutual fund company and let them know you want to sell your shares.

INVESTOR TRIVIA

Got Junk?

Very risky bonds are often called junk bonds. These bonds pay a high rate of interest, but there is also a good chance that the company that borrows the money will not be able to pay it back. Because of their unpredictability, most serious investors stay away from junk bonds despite their high rate of return.

You will receive a check from the company for the value of the shares you are redeeming at the price they were worth on the day your request was received. Some expenses may be deducted from this amount (see below).

Like all investments, mutual funds also have their downsides. For one, the securities contained within a mutual fund can be volatile—their values rise and fall. If the stock market experiences a free fall, then your mutual funds may also decrease in value. For example, if technology stocks decrease in value, mutual funds holding a lot of stocks in that sector will most likely lose value as well. If you redeem shares for less than what you paid for them, you will lose money. Most people do not like the idea of losing money. If the thought of losing money upsets you, think seriously about whether or not a mutual fund is the right investment for you. You might want to look instead at savings accounts or other investments offered by a bank, like certificates of deposit (CDs). Although they don't typically perform as well as mutual funds, these accounts are very safe.

Another disadvantage of a mutual fund is that you may have to pay income tax on the money it generates. Income, whether earned from employment or an investment, is taxable. If you are still a dependent, then someone else, like a parent or caregiver, is claiming you on their yearly federal and state tax returns. This person might be the one who is responsible for paying the income tax on your investment. If you file your own tax return, you could see a decrease in the amount of your tax refund (if you receive one) when you redeem your shares because you will be taxed on the money the mutual fund earned. The income you earn from mutual funds is taxed at a lower rate than regular income. You should check with a qualified income tax consultant about how to report income and pay the taxes on money earned by a mutual fund.

Some mutual fund companies invest in tax-free municipal bonds, and therefore are able to offer tax-free mutual funds. But despite being labeled tax-free, these investments may still require the payment of some taxes. Capital gains taxes may be owed if you sell your shares at a higher NAV than they were purchased at, or if capital gains distributions are made. In addition, tax-free mutual funds usually earn less than taxed mutual funds. Depending on your tax bracket, you could actually end up earning less money, not more, when you invest in a tax-free mutual fund.

There are some expenses involved in purchasing any mutual fund. While it is possible to purchase a no-load mutual fund, all funds have some expenses that are passed on to their investors. The fund manager is paid for administering the fund. Other expenses are business related, like printing fund literature and mailing it, and paying for legal advice, if needed. These expenses are taken out of the investors' profits. The higher the expenses, the less profit investors make. Since hundreds or thousands of people may be invested in the same mutual fund, all expenses are divided among all the people who own the fund. Still, in order to maximize their profit, many investors seek out low-cost funds, like the T. Rowe Price Growth Stock Fund and the Fidelity Blue Chip Growth Fund. These funds, and others like them, try to keep their operating expenses below 1 percent of their holdings. Nevertheless, any charges to buy or sell shares, as well as the operating costs, should be thoroughly researched before you make an investment in any mutual fund.

You've developed a financial plan, learned all you can about investments, and decided on a portfolio of investments. Why are you still sitting on your money? It's time to invest!

CHAPTER 5

Let's Invest Some MONEY!

Ready to invest in a mutual fund? Taking a look at a mutual fund prospectus will help you decide if a mutual fund is the right investment for you. Every mutual fund publishes a prospectus. If a prospectus contains information that you do not understand, be sure to ask for help before you invest.

What is the objective or goal of the mutual fund? This section tells a prospective investor what the mutual fund hopes to accomplish, and whether it is a growth fund which should be kept for years, or a short-term, income-producing fund.

What investment strategies does the fund use? What type of securities does the mutual fund invest in? As a possible investor, you will want to know not only the type of securities the mutual fund presently invests in, but also the economic sector the securities belong to. You will also want to know the portfolio turnover—or how often the fund buys and sells securities.

Always understand the risks involved before you place your money in an investment.

What are the risks of investing in this particular mutual fund? Make sure the risk of the investment matches your comfort level. If you can't afford to risk your money, you may want to look into a safer investment.

How can shares of the fund be purchased and redeemed? Some funds must be purchased through a licensed broker, but most can be purchased directly from the mutual fund company. How can shares be redeemed? Is there a cost associated with either purchasing or redeeming shares of the fund?

Who is the portfolio manager? A prospectus will provide the name and address of the portfolio manager and the financial credentials and experience that make him or her qualified to manage the fund.

A mutual fund prospectus is an invaluable means of learning all you can about the fund you are thinking of investing in.

What is the fund's history? A mutual fund must detail its history over the last ten years, if it has been in existence this long, so that possible investors can see how well it has done. If the fund isn't yet ten years old, the report must give the history for the years the fund has been in existence. Look at the fund's rate of return to see how well the fund is performing. How long has the portfolio manager or team been with the fund? The performance of the fund over the last ten years might not mean much if the current manager has only been managing the fund for the past year. Also consider the performance of the fund in relation to the overall market. What happened to the fund at times when the market wasn't doing so well?

What is the shareholder's tax responsibility? Remember, even if an investment is labeled "tax-free," this doesn't mean it truly is.

What are the expenses of the mutual fund? What expenses and fees will be deducted from the profits of the mutual fund? How will these fees affect the fund's earnings over time?

Confucius was an ancient Chinese philosopher who is famous for sharing his wisdom on many topics, including money management and investments.

The ancient philosopher Confucius (551 BCE–479 BCE) proved he knew something about investing when he said: "If a little money does not go out, great money will not come in." Every investor must decide for himself or herself when is the right time to invest a "little money." And the "great money"? If you plan, do your research, and keep on top of your investments, there is a very good chance that "great money" will one day come to you!

INVESTOR TRIVIA

Spiders? Diamonds?
ETFs that track the performance of the S&P 500 are nicknamed spiders. ETFs that track the Dow Jones Industrial Average, which follows thirty blue-chip stocks, are called diamonds.

Twenty Largest Mutual Fund Companies
with contact information and sampling of fund types

American Century Investments	AmericanCentury.com (800) 345-2021	Growth, technology, and industrial stock funds; municipal bond funds; money market funds.
American Funds	AmericanFunds.com (800) 421-4225	Growth, international, industrial, and healthcare stock funds; bond funds.
BlackRock	BlackRock.com	Value, growth, financial, healthcare, and energy stock funds; bond funds.
Columbia Management	ColumbiaManagement. com (800) 345-6611	Growth, international, index, technology, and industrial stock funds; municipal bond funds.
Dimensional	DFAUS.com (512) 306-7400	Value, international, industrial, and financial stock funds.
Dodge & Cox	DodgeandCox.com (800) 621-3979	Value, global, international, income, technology, financial, healthcare, and energy stock funds; bond funds.
Fidelity Investments	Fidelity.com (800) 343-3548	Value, growth, global, international, index, technology, financial, and consumer stock funds; municipal and Treasury bond funds; money market funds.
Franklin Templeton Investments	FranklinTempleton.com (800) 632-2301	Value, growth, global, international, financial, healthcare, and energy stock funds; precious metal funds; municipal and tax-free bond funds.
Invesco	Invesco.com (800) 959-4246	Value, growth, technology, financial, and healthcare stock funds; bond funds.
Janus	Janus.com (800) 525-3713	Growth, global, international, and income stock funds; bond funds; money market funds.
John Hancock	JohnHancock.com (800) 225-5291	Growth, international, income, technology, financial, and consumer stock funds; bond funds.
J.P. Morgan Asset Management	JPMorganFunds.com (800) 480-4111	Value, growth, global, international, technology, financial, and consumer stock funds; government and tax-free bond funds.

Legg Mason Global Asset Management	Leggmason.com (800) 822-5544	Value, growth, international, technology, financial, and healthcare stock funds; government, tax-free and bond funds; money market funds.
MFS Investment Management	MFS.com (800) 225-2606	Value, growth, global, income, industrial, and financial stock funds; municipal and tax-free bonds; money market funds.
Oppenheimer Funds	OppenheimerFunds.com (888) 470-0862	Value, growth, income, global, international, income, technology, financial, and consumer stock funds; precious metal funds; municipal, government, and corporate bond funds; money market funds.
PIMCO Funds	Investments.Pimco.com (888) 877-4626	Global and income stock funds; ETFs; municipal and government bond funds; money market funds.
Principal Financial Group	Principal.com (800) 222-5852	Value, international, financial, and real estate stock funds; government bond funds.
The Vanguard Group	Vanguard.com (877) 662-7447	Growth, income, index, technology, healthcare, and energy stock funds; precious metal funds; ETFs; municipal, tax-free, Treasury, and corporate bond funds; money market funds.
T. Rowe Price	TRowePrice.com (800) 638-5660	Growth, global, international, income, technology, healthcare, and consumer stock funds; international, municipal, tax-free and Treasury bond funds.
Wells Fargo Advantage Funds	WellsFargoAdvantageFunds. com (800) 359-3379	Value, growth, international, income, index, technology, and consumer stock funds; municipal and government bond funds; money market funds.

LOW COST MUTUAL FUNDS TO CONSIDER

Vanguard

FUND	Annual Fund Operating Expense	FUND MANAGER
500 Index Fund Investor Shares (VFINX)	0.17%	Portfolio Manager Michael H. Buek, CFA, Principal of Vanguard.
California Intermediate Term Tax Exempt Investors Shares (VCAIX)	0.20%	James M. D'Arcy, CFA, Portfolio Manager.
Vanguard Equity Income (VEIPX)	0.30%	W. Michael Reckmeyer, III, Wellington Management Company
Vanguard Dividend Growth (VDIGX)	0.31%	Donald J. Kilbride, Wellington Management Company
Vanguard Short-Term Bond Index Fund Investor Shares (VBISX)	0.20%	Kenneth E. Volpert, CFA, Principal of Vanguard and head of Vanguard's Taxable Bond Group. Joshua C. Barrickman, CFA, Principal of Vanguard and head of Vanguard's Bond Index Group.
Wellesley Income (VWINX)	0.25%	John C. Keogh, Wellington Management Company
Wellington Fund (VWELX)	0.25%	Edward P. Bousa, CFA, Senior Vice President and Equity Portfolio Manager of Wellington Management. John C. Keogh, Senior Vice President and Fixed Income Portfolio Manager of Wellington Management.

Fidelity

FUND	Annual Fund Operating Expense	FUND MANAGER
Fidelity Growth Discovery Fund (FDSVX)	0.81%	Jason Weiner (portfolio manager)
Fidelity Low –priced Stock Fund (FLPSX)	0.88%	Jamie Harmon, Justin Bennett, and others
Rydex Government Long Bond (RYGBX)	0.95%	Michael P. Byrum , CFA, Mike Dellapa , CFA, CAIA and others
Wasatch-Hoisington U.S. Treasury Fund (WHOSX)	0.75%	Van R. Hoisington
Goldman Sachs Investment Grade Credit Fund Class A (GSGAX)	0.85%	Lale Topcuoglu, Ben Johnson
American Century Investments Zero Coupon 2020 Fund Investor Class (BTTX)	0.55%	Brian Howell, James Platz, Robert Gahagan

T. Rowe Price

FUND	Annual Fund Operating Expense	FUND MANAGER
Blue Chip Growth Fund (TRPCX)	0.76%	Larry J. Puglia Chairman of Investment Advisory Committee
Capital Appreciation Fund (PRWCX)	0.72%	David R. Giroux, Chairman, and others
Equity Income Fund (PRFDX)	0.68%	Brian C. Rogers Chairman of Investment Advisory Committee
California Tax Free Bond Fund (PRXCX)	0.51%	Konstantine B. Mallas Chairman of Investment Advisory Committee
Corporate Income Fund (PRPIX)	0.51%	David A. Tiberii Chairman of Investment Advisory Committee
Financial Services Fun (PRISX)	0.94%	Eric L. Veiel Chairman of Investment Advisory Committee

* This is not a recommendation to purchase. It is a place you can start your research for your own portfolio.

Carroll, Adam, and Chad Carden. *Winning The Money Game: A Rule Book to Achieving Financial Success for Young People.* Clive, Iowa: National Financial Educators, 2006.

Radden, Viki. *The Money Tree: The Young People's Illustrated Guide to Saving, Banking, and Investing.* Scotts Valley, California: CreateSpace Independent Publishing Platform, 2012.

Stahl, Michael. *Early to Rise: A Young Adult's Guide to Saving, Investing and Financial Decisions that Can Shape Your Life.* Aberdeen, Washington: Silver Lake Publishing, 2005.

Wolpert, Edward M. *The Young Adult's Guide to Financial Success.* Decatur, Georgia: Oconee Financial Planning Services LLC, 2009.

On the Internet

Investopedia: "Mutual Funds & ETFs"
http://www.investopedia.com/investing/mutual-funds-and-etfs/
Morningstar
http://www.morningstar.com
Teens Guide to Money: "Mutual Funds"
http://www.teensguidetomoney.com/investing/mutual-funds/
The Motley Fool: "Teens and Their Money"
http://www.fool.com/teens/teens01.htm

Berg, Stacie Zoe. *The Unofficial Guide to Investing in Mutual Funds.* New York: Macmillan USA, 1999.

Bresiger, Gregory. "Precious Metal Funds: A Golden Opportunity?" Investopedia, November 17, 2012. http://www.investopedia.com/articles/mutualfund/09/precious-metals-funds.asp#axzz2Gf29r5IA

"Explaining Stocks and the Stock Market." CNN Money. http://money.cnn.com/magazines/moneymag/money101/lesson5/index2.htm

Gremillion, Lee L. *Mutual Fund Industry Handbook: A Comprehensive Guide for Investment Professionals.* Hoboken, New Jersey: John Wiley & Sons, 2005.

"Index Investing: Index Funds." Investopedia, 2012. http://www.investopedia.com/university/indexes/index8.asp#axzz2NAjxSDKu

"Introduction to Money Market Mutual Funds." Investopedia, September 10, 2010. http://www.investopedia.com/articles/mutualfund/04/081104.asp#axzz2CdW2GEsM

Kansas, Dave. "What is a Bond?" *The Wall Street Journal.* http://guides.wsj.com/personal-finance/investing/what-is-a-bond

MarksJarvis, Gail. "Saving for Retirement: Start Investing Early, or Start Now." *Financial Times,* September 21, 2007. http://www.ftpress.com/articles/article.aspx?p=707401

Mintzer, Rich, and Barry Littmann. *The Everything Mutual Funds Book: How to Pick, Buy, and Sell Mutual Funds and Watch Your Money Grow!* Holbrook, Massachusetts: Adams Media, 2000.

Mobius, Mark. *Mutual Funds: An Introduction to the Core Concepts.* Singapore: John Wiley & Sons, 2007.

Northcott, Alan. *The Mutual Funds Book: How to Invest in Mutual Funds & Earn High Rates of Returns Safely.* Ocala, Florida: Atlantic Publishing Co., 2008.

Scott, David. L. *Investing in Mutual Funds.* Boston: Houghton-Mifflin Harcourt, 2004.

Taulli, Tom. "4 Low-cost, High Performance Mutual Funds." InvestorPlace, April 27, 2012. http://investorplace.com/2012/04/4-low-cost-high-performance-mutual-funds/

"The Money 70." *Money Magazine.* January/February 2012, p. 122.

Tyson, Eric. *Mutual Funds for Dummies.* Hoboken, New Jersey: Wiley Publishing, 2010.

Updegrave, Walter. "Are Money-market Accounts and Funds the Same?" CNN Money, June 13, 2012. http://money.cnn.com/2012/06/13/pf/expert/money-market-funds.moneymag/index.htm

Williamson, Gordon K. *The 100 Best Mutual Funds You Can Buy 2001.* Holbrook, Massachusetts: Adams Media Corporation, 2000.

asset (AS-et): something of value such as cash, securities, machinery, or real estate

bond: an investment in which the investor loans money to a corporation or government in exchange for a set interest rate

blue-chip stock: low-risk stock of a large, established company which often pays dividends

broker: an agent who sells products and receives a fee or commission for his or her services

commodity (kuh-MOD-i-tee): a product that is traded widely, usually of uniform quality, such as salt, oil, or gold

default (dih-FAWLT): a failure to meet an obligation, such as repayment of a debt

dependent (dih-PEN-duhnt): a person who relies on another person for basic needs

economy (ih-KON-uh-mee): the money, jobs, production, and management of resources by a community or country

growth fund: a type of mutual fund that invests in rapidly growing companies instead of established, dividend-paying companies

interest rate (IN-ter-ist REYT): the amount of money paid for the use of the money, expressed as an annual percentage

liability (lahy-uh-BIL-i-tee): money owed

net asset value (NET AS-et VAL-yoo): the price per share of a mutual fund, calculated by adding the value of all securities in the portfolio, minus expenses, divided by the number of shares; also known as NAV

real estate (REEL ih-STEYT): land, the air above it, and the buildings and structures on it

redeem (ri-DEEM): to convert back to cash; sell

sector (SEK-ter): an industry or market within the economy, like healthcare, technology, or real estate

security (si-KYOOR-i-tee): any of a number of types of investments, including stocks and bonds

stock: partial ownership of a company

value fund (VAL-yoo FUHND): a type of mutual fund that invests in undervalued companies that pay dividends

volatile (VOL-uh-til): extremely changeable

About the
AUTHOR

Marylou Morano Kjelle is a college English professor and freelance writer who lives and works in Central New Jersey. She has written dozens of books for young readers of all ages, many for Mitchell Lane Publishers. Marylou holds M.S. and M.A. degrees. When she is not teaching or writing, Marylou gardens, cooks, and bakes for her family, watches movies, and reads as many books as she possibly can.